Mind–Heart–Soul Connection and People

Mind-Heart-Soul Connection and People

John Kaufman

Blue Ink Media Solutions

Mind-Heart-Soul Connection and People

Copyright © 2024 by John Kaufman. All rights reserved.

No part of this publication may be reproduced, distributed, or transmitted in any form or by any means, including photocopying, recording, or other electronic or mechanical methods, without the prior written permission of the author, except in the case of brief quotations embodied in critical reviews and certain other noncommercial uses permitted by copyright law.

The contents of this work, including, but not limited to, the accuracy of events, people, and places depicted; opinions expressed; permission to use previously published materials included; and any advice given or actions advocated are solely the responsibility of the author, who assumes all liability for said work and indemnifies the publisher against any claims stemming from publication of the work.

Printed in the United States of America
ISBN 978-1-64133-979-7 (hc)
ISBN 978-1-64133-980-3 (sc)
ISBN 978-1-64133-981-0 (e)

2024.11.07

This book is printed on acid-free paper.

Because of the dynamic nature of the Internet, any web addresses or links contained in this book may have changed since publication and may no longer be valid. The views expressed in this work are solely those of the author and do not necessarily reflect the views of the publisher, and the publisher hereby disclaims any responsibility for them.

Blue Ink Media Solutions
1111B S Governors Ave
STE 7582 Dover,
DE 19904

www.blueinkmediasolutions.com

Table of Contents

Introduction 1
Sanctity in our Speaking 2
Author's Comment 3
The Serenade 4
Food For Thought 6
Mirror, Mirror on the Wall 7
Mind-Boggling Bad Assumptions 8
Spaghetti Don't Mind if I Do 10
Breathe Normally Please 12
Incessant Ringing of the Bells 14
Solid Dark Chocolate 16
I Cannot Imagine My Life Without Pets! 19
In Memory of All Those Beloved Pets Lost Each Year 20
Just Scratching the Surface 21
Just a Thought 22
At the End of Your Ropes 23
The American Wasteland 25
Stupidity 26
Money-money-money 27
Here is a Sad Story 29
Somewhere a Place 30
Rabbit Stew 31
Dam-it, the Rabbit! 33
Walking a Thin Line 34
Mental Health 36
Anti-depressants or Anti-pills 37
Vanilla or Chocolate 39

No One Changes 40
The Problem with Free Thinking... 41
Guilty or More Guilty.. 42
Let's Pretend.. 43
A Christmas Without Santa 45
Life is Like the Cactus... 47
Undying Love 48
From Here to Nowhere 49
Stupidity and the Soul... 50
Mr. Fix-It! 51
A Letter With a Junk Store Cat 53
A Happy Birthday Poem for My Aunt Ardis 55
Happy Birthday, Dad 57
Birthday-Cake-Ice-Cream-Mom 58
Goodnight for Christmas.. 60
Stuff to Consider!.. 62
The Lessons of Self.. 63
An Unloving Family Will Always Equal Loneliness! 64
Sounds of Random Negativity 65
Sun Bleached Bones 66
Fifty Years and Counting.. 67
The Rest of Your Life... 69
The Soul-Spiritual-Connection 71
None of My Business 72
One Hundred Percent Organic 74
Eyes of an Old Dog.. 76
Domination 77
The Monkey and the Snake 78
To Love or Not to Love... 79
More Food for Thought 80
Joy Robbers...81
My Dark Twisted Jungle 82
Pocket Full of Coupons... 84
The Scorpion and the Turtle 86
Messages From God 87

Introduction

Listening to the constant clamoring noise of my mind-heart-soul connection has become an obsession in my thoughts and chinking. Unclear images, and the relentless noise of the past, can overshadow and darken the path through one's life. Regardless of want or motivation, living in disconnectedness, over time, will become corrosive, often resulting in becoming mentally ill inherited from lack of any mind-heart-soul connection, that place where the good in humanity survives and triumphs over the bad. Believe it or not.

We can only concern ourselves with our future by giving our souls what it needs today. Remember to tend to your souls spirit. Like any successful garden, the need begins when you consciously commit to having a garden, neglected or otherwise, from that beginning to its dying natural end. After which, in your hereafter, you will be rewarded by reaping what you had in a lifetime sown.

Unless you hear and see your soul, the murmurs of your past, those silent cries of darkened souls, will continue to invalidate you and your existence. So much loss of mind-heart-soul can take away any joys of inexperienced glory in life. One' s beingness can live in a world where humanity's brain-heart is in a battle over how to survive death without a meaningful, healthy acknowledgment of the crucial vital importance of the eternity of your soul.

Sanctity in our Speaking

With all the division in the world today, global warming, the war in Ukraine, hunger, homelessness, water shortages, and on God like hatred corning from the minds-hearts-souls of humanity. We continually wait and hope, hoping and waiting for the cruel world to become a place where the sanctity of speaking truths still rules. If the planet's humanity becomes hopeless, it would be my prediction that we are doomed to live in a world that eventually will become more hopelessly doomed. Like so many, knowing it did not have to turn out this way. The complete distinction of any "mind-heart-soul connections," will become a losing battle directly caused by humanity's relationship with truth, compassion, and understanding; losing what we once thought to be unthinkable: the lack of any conscious or unconscious relationships, one soulless inhabitant that, like so many others, never missed their souls to begin with.

If there is a heaven, it cries out for God, whoever it be, to intervene in a world of people created in his supposed image, such likeness offered to reflect somehow the mind, heart, and lose souls, humanity's failures showing up in all of us.

So many of us live and die without holding tight onto those things we should love, including our soul, and the miraculous possibility of all human life, and after our death, we can live through our souls' birth and rebirth—our individual soul's ascension.

Author's Comment

This work of arc was created with my devotion to the brain-heart- soul connection. le is my intentions to satisfy my soul's need to communicate with humanity in a conversation of the transformational power of having a three-dimensional soul. The seeds I plane are from my collection. Harvested throughout my life of living, and hope you find a place in your mind-heart-soul to feel the emotions in my work, that is good for humanity's health. Here's to all those who seek eternity through a loving living soul.

The Serenade

In serenade I searched for love,
I sang with crazy foolish pride.
With any great lover's quest,
some will always be denied.

There has never been a love song,
true feeling sang from the heart.
With hope comes expectations,
a natural place to scare.

I woo some elusive vision,
even when I am depressed and blue.
For if I died at this moment,
it would be in search of you!

Those love songs went unanswered,
left deep scars in one's foolish pride.
A lonely heart yearns for someone,
to brighten the years of dreary skies.

Then one day when I was singing,
perched under a bright blue sky.
The songs that I had been singing,
gone unanswered, not a single reply?

The years gone by, I've stopped singing,
no call of the wild in my lonely days.
Yet I will forever remember singing,
my perfect serenade.

This is a poem about love, hopes, dreams, and unfilled intentions.

Food For Thought

Every soul often becomes lonely and needs a bit of recognition, donations of any amount, light up a dark soul with ocher's generosity.

What is life without the gift of mind-heart-soul-connections? Disconnected, repetitive unconsciousness that leaves you to hopelessly play the game of life with your face stacked against you.

The mind's consciousness and unconscious manipulated by the appropriate amount of mind-heart-soul balance is what humanity so desperately needs.

Mirror, Mirror on the Wall

A healthy mind-heart connection can only begin when you stand in front of yourself and spend some time having the contents of your soul reflect on you.

The gardener's plot of land on this earth is solely unlimited.

In darkness can come light. Humanity's souls believe.

Unless we give ourselves a loving soul, it has no opinion of our choices. If it becomes small and insignificant, it will be there for you. Standing by you through your lifetime of unhappiness, bitterness, and every mile you've gone, noticed or not, each of our souls has far more patience and love stowed away, regardless if you see little value in that cargo.

{Songs of faith sung by the choir.}

Preaching to ourselves and loved ones, including those singing in the choir, often don't harvest the value of a kind heart, a forgiving mind, and a beautiful soul's importance. Those with logical retrospect can foresee their future by looking at their past and change the course to avoid the crash, die and burn syndrome scenario that can't end well. Never really becoming a mind-heart-soul kind of person will without any intention not spare you from becoming a *Humpty-Dumpty* kind of soul, that can never be put back together again.

The difference among all great recipes starts with the success of those who gave it to you, great taste as well as enlightenment has to have started somewhere.

Mind-Boggling Bad Assumptions

Suppose we could dig up the remnants of all past lives from man's earliest beginning, those people who made up the human race. The number of souls that have departed God's planet, earth, is mind-boggling.

This book exposes one mind's creativity. It is an inside look at a man that believes in something even when there is nothing to believe in!

When you fail, you know what wise men say? Try, try, try again until you succeed!

That could be twisted advice. If every boat you try to construct never floats, stop trying. You are not a boat maker kind of person.

There's nothing wrong with getting things right except all those things you mostly don't get right.

The truth you search for is often found in your relationship with your soul and who you choose to be. Sometimes, coo many trial and errors come from how your brain works with you or against you without input from a good heart and the guidance of a well-maintained soul.

We intuitively know we are responsible for plotting a successful path throughout our God-given life. The destination becomes unclear when the mind, heart, and soul show signs of losing hope, faith, and joy.

You begin to be like all those other wandering nomads, lost in a life with no destiny. Living life inside our ever-darkening void becomes a soul's death sentence. Any possibility of life after death is significantly diminished if you are dead in mind and heart long before you are forced to board that train you chose to nowhere.

When we stop following the call of eternity, the destination may be inconsequential and disappointing; with the possibility of a glorious afterlife would not be your final destiny. Ie will be a tragic final destination, ending nowhere.

Dumb-Di-Dum-Dum!

Spaghetti Don't Mind if I Do

Let me sympathize with those of us that struggle with many times feeling stupid. So many times, I've stopped counting! I am left with dear images. My picturesque, complete color memory recall makes my mind, heart, and soul chuckle whenever I need to amuse myself with funny thoughts on going throughout my long life.

{Sounds of a wedding reception celebration}

I stood in line, waiting to serve myself from a banquet table with people walking down both sides of the cable and picking up their silverware, napkin, and a large plate. I was always nervous, among others, and my anxiety always caused me to feel like a pig farmer that smelled of the farm. If you have a good soul, there is nothing wrong with being a pig farmer or anything else. We are who and what we are. At this moment, I found myself picking up a big plate. I stood in front of a humongous bowl of spaghetti with tongs. I succeeded in putting a generous portion of pasta on my plate. Next came an enormous metal container with red spaghetti sauce and a giant ladle hanging inside the massive sauce pot. With my dinner plate loaded with Italian noodles, now swimming in brilliantly bright red, rich tomato sauce, I, to my best recollection, remember returning the ladle to the oversized metal sauce container. I moved on. Not very far down the table, I saw people loo kin g at me with those looks you receive when making a fool out of yourself. Somehow the big ladle's hooked-end had caught on my coat sleeve and was hanging from my right arm full of sauce! Now I had moved some distance down the banquet line, not realizing as I moved, I was swinging sauce to the right of me, to the left of me. Ie was, at best, a dicey situation, as I could see people quietly laughing and pointing at me from the other side of the table. My mind went to overload. I am trying to remember what I did with the ladle and who cleaned up the mess afterward. I don't know. The last thing I remember was looking down at my new shiny shoes, completely shellacked in red spaghetti sauce. Not just my dress shoes; the tomato sauce was on the long dresses of those on both sides of me. The important thing for all of us is to learn. The brain will begin to overlook life's mistakes if you allow the heart and soul to be comforted by the strength that a healthy mindheart-soul connection provides. We are all human, and if we are lucky, we will have much to laugh about as we grow older, laughing at ourselves, those times that make us feel stupid. That now makes me laugh.

Breathe Normally Please

I've heard that request coo many times in the past three hundred years. I was always high-strung with anxiety issues, and I never learned to breathe normally. I was one of those overly hyper-active kids who always chased some thin g. In my case, I had no idea what that was. Most days until I became utterly unconscious and worn out. My breathing changed tempo as much as the disorder I was suffering. My mind's conversations that kept me years later still caught in the aftermath of life's storms. Unknowingly at that time, I was safely tethered to my connection of mind-heart-soul which in time became a staunch protector of me. Most importantly my soul was what had kept my mind from destroying my heart. Many times the balance of soul lies within the boundaries of one's heart.

All of "us" who somehow survived a lifetime of anxiety tend to feel helpless in the struggles of those strong undercurrents drowning the soul from lack of air, day in and day out.

I have always been interested in the "life of my mental illness." Authentic, open, and always honest. What do you want to know? It's my way of talking about mental illness. "Us!" It describes the chronic conditions of most folks in today's changing world, insanely individual, mainly when referring to souls so full of rips and tears and overflowing with too many voids. Having needs left unattended will change people's ability to think with a mind-heart-soul allowing those of us to show up as shining multi-dimensional-beings.

The most dangerous aspect can be one's thinking. Most people, day after day, are mentally in conflict. Mind-heart and soul will always reflect inwardly. The enemy is not what you're thinking if you are unable to think. Nor is it your heart if you are rather heartless. You are quickly pointing the finger at the soul. It must be your good-for nothing, hard-to -look-at, miserable soul.

{Dark musty smells at a miserable-souls convention.}

Incessant Ringing of the Bells

The inescapable fact is that we live, die, and in between, we go through the process of living and dying depending on one's particular orientation somewhere between being alive and being pronounced dead.

With the constant clanging of the bells, how does one disregard the noise in which they hear no music? Ear pods, earphones, ear muffs, earwigs, along vacation? Figure it out; you are mor e intelligent than a bunch of useless ringing bells.

{Muffled so und of annoying bells ringing}

On the topic of God-religion-soul, I do not believe that souls need much of anything. You are conceived with a soul that will exist till your death. Souls are much like a sponge, and they're absorbent, clean up head-heart, and hard to get at places.

All souls have a departing destination on the Soul Train to the hereafter, a magnificent ride to your eternity. Wait, as I have noted throughout my writings. Trains, it seems, have more than one destination. When planning that inevitable future journey, plan well in advance. Being conscious of tending to life's garden brings forth the light that can shine through one's soul. A soul that had been prepared for all eternity. Believe It or not!

There is always less potential in seeing nothing than the possibilities you make out of that nothingness.

Climbing every mountain and your imagination will ultimately get you to the top. Being old and tired has nothing to do with our eternal spirit, and it will only soar far beyond those places you did nor climb. When it bids you farewell—departing filled with the beauty of what you had planted. A garden that will in the end prove we reap what we sow.

John Kaufman - November 20, 2022

Solid Dark Chocolate

Easter is for rabbits,
the kind that likes to hop,
while they gather Easter eggs,
from all their favorite spots.

Spring is in the garden,
and the flowers love lots of sunlight,
where each single rabbit will be,
an Easter bunny tonight.

They eat their carrots early in the day,
it's energy for the job,
delivering marsh mellow chickens,
in baskets filled with artificial sod.

All the little chicks,
that are big enough to help,
paint their mother's eggs with care,
and put chem on the shelf.

The work started a year ago,
to make this da y just right,
for Easter is a special time,
each basket a glorious delight.

I hope the Easter bunny,
I saw hopping off your way,
delivered you an Easter basket,
on this special day.

I hope it had some chocolate eggs,
filled with decadent cream and nuts,
with decorated colored eggs,
laid from all those amazing butts.

For all their work and effort,
those chickens laid more than a few,
think about those little chicks,
painting eggs yellow, pink, and blue.

Plenty of eggs got busted,
lucky no workers' butts got beat,
some baskets were not ready,
and some were not complete.

But most of the work got handled,
and most works got done,
it kept them all very busy,
each and every one .

So, if you got an Easter basket,
and the job done was not quite right,
some little Easter bunny is sorry,
feeling terrible tonight.

Tomorrow, in the garden,
with all those bunny treats,
there will be an Easter party,
with lots of scuff to eat.

The chicks and their mothers,
back doing what chickens do,
the rabbits all paired up with one another,
doing that bunny dance for two.

With love and all best wishes,
I send this Easter thought;
here's hoping all your Easter bunnies,
are solid dark Choc-Co-lore.

John Kaufman - 1996

I Cannot Imagine My Life Without Pets!

Looking back on all those precious moments,
that are forever etched deeply in my hardwood floors.
Problem with pets, I ask myself thoughts I just ignore,
as I watch them scratching off molding around doors.

We can sometimes be too needy,
in need of others' endearing, loving care.
I wake up each morning with a mouth
full of my pets dogs' and cats' hair.

I never found very much joy or happiness,
in dating wild women or chasing pretty boys.
It's understood my money now goes mostly
to fancy pee foods and annoying, squeaky toys.

For all those days to me rain or shine,
comforted by pure animal devotion.
A life filled with so much lovely attention,
all my past pet's names I wish to mention.

Carmen, Cody, Baby-Girl, TJ, JJ,
Kitty-Kitty, Rascal, Tomm y-Boy, Susie, Marley,
Martha, Kahuna, T ripper, Charlie, Jordan,
Cry-Baby, and Chicken-Hawk to name a few.

In Memory of All Those Beloved Pets Lost Each Year

Hearts filled with grief, the forever joyous sorrow.

A best friend named Tippi

I was five years old and my dog Tippi was by my side. We were walking on the side of a dusty gravel road. It was great, just my dog and me. I never felt unloved or alone when we were together. Tip pi had a bad habit of chasing cars. It was no different this day, except he would not be coming home this time. fu the car sped by, it was engulfed with the dust it was kicking up. I watched as my dog and best friend rolled end over end, landing by the side of the road covered in blood . I, in desperation, began crying and screaming to anyone who might hear that I needed band aids.

In so many days of my life, I prayed for band-aids. Band-aids for all my beloved adored pets that never fixed my broken heart by applying pretty colorful parches.

John Kaufman - November 29, 2022

Just Scratching the Surface

They are now randomly scratching everything. I am assuming they are bored. With one of so many pets no one singular pet is to blame! I don't care about it very much. I always had pets to comfort me. Love always comes with a few chores. They surround ed me with love strengthening my commitment to the extra tasks it takes to be this blessed.

Just a Thought

What fools are we to n ever look at all the possibilities and then choose? It would be like spending all your money before you get to town.

At the End of Your Ropes

I share my deepest despair at that place where there seems to be nothing to hang onto. Ie would be self-serving to tether all the rope ends you spend your days dinging, hands-on fire from all those painful rope burns. How long had it been since your thinking mind became overgrown and tangled in life's attempts to stop eying restrictive knots in the little amount of rope we have left to lose foolishly.

All those times you struggled, your right-fisted grips slowly starred tearing at your hands, and your mind too often began to slip away.

When consciously distracted by your unconscious thinking, your mind-heart-soul connections may be tenuous behavior that you need to focus more on.

You want to run, to run to some different place. Only all those ropes lack the knowledge to listen to your voice, telling you what you cannot bring yourself to hear.

Disparity ends at a time and a place where and when one commies to leaving it. Letting go of some of our wrong and unhealthy behaviors is much more successful with conscious, supportive attention—a Three-Dimensional-Soul can better support your emotional needs, wants, and likes with a better perspective and add purpose to life. Better-connected, happier person.

Like an accomplished puppeteer, he is aware of those strings he must pull at any given moment in his performance. You need those ropes to dance if you are the puppet. But when tied to lines that are not supporting our activities, we are lost and ignorant of understanding what we try hard to see in ourselves but never do!

When you find yourself in a crowd surrounded by people, feeling lonely, it's not you; it's the crowd!

I often had to tell myself lonely comes from the lack of goodwill in the air. My mind-heart-soul long ago knew I survived by having a threedimensional soul which always I relied upon.

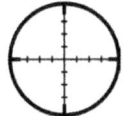

The American Wasteland

{Maddening Sounds of a Soulless World}

I was digging as if there was somewhere to go! I was caught unprepared in my moment when the acid-laden heavens above corrosively ate away any resemblance of the humanity I would, without choice, leave behind.

The times they are a-changing was just an old expression that died when the world began systematically being inoculated from itself.

Now it was my turn to shed my human identity. As time passed, I managed to stay alive, never losing sight of my innate intentions to survive, somehow, live the rest of my life without a soul, soulless!

Even now, l was rapidly distracted by my mind's rapid intrusion of explosions of the organisms aggressively changing me and the world in which I muse now live!

I felt no reluctance! Instead, I fully embraced what I was biologically becoming—one of the thousand or so remaining humans to cross over. A world in which mind-heart-soul had no importance, a world that has so little consciousness of what humanity lost.

Stupidity

It's not how smart you are! It's how dumb you feel, like us all, we can tend to be too hard on ourselves, given we are only human!

IQ, like your weight, does not matter; dumbness and pant sizes are optional. Smart or dumb, souls come in all shapes, weights, and shades of brilliance in their afterlife.

Money-money-money

One day an older man in the community attended a Sunday morning church service. He was well-known by everyone near and far. But he had not been much of a churchgoer. This day he was in attendance. It was a time for the minister to give thanks as the ushers took their places, ready for them to collect those Sunday tidings. In his prayer, he lee everyone in heaven and those churchgoers in each Sunday sermon he preached, reminding them of all the construction and improvements going on to their once inefficient small place of worship with many of its skyrocketing costs. In the background, the choir softly sang an old gospel hymn, "Bringing in the Sheaves."

Immediately after the service had ended, on that memorable church-blessed day. Two gentlemen approached a man who had written a check made out to the church for one hundred thousand dollars! They came to the older man who had been so generous, and he was asked if this might be a joke. It was no joke, and the works in progress were soon completed.

I knew about this man's generous contribution, and many years had passed. I asked him how he now felt about donating one hundred thousand dollars of his hard-earned money to the church. He answered, they soon forget!

Every soul wants to feel worthy. The soul becomes lonely and in need of recognition. Donations of any amount may start to make the soul doubt the rewards it has been working towards.

Suppose you are that person feeling lost and lonely in a crowd. Avoid significant gatherings filled with an audience so big that nobody listens to your need for attention.

All things become new again when being guided by a renewal in your mind-heart-soul connection.

All those beautiful souls that are wandering through their lifetime of lost time, having been foolish enough to ignore the mind-heart- soul connection. You will be left, forever, searching for a needle in the wrong haystack. Your soul could be assumed lost and feared dark going unnoticed.

Here is a Sad Story

Being a creative type of soul, I write stories about almost anything. Pets included! Here's a dedicated tale to all of us over-indulgent lovers of pets.

My family and I lived on a gravel road on a modest dairy furn. About a half mile or so was the Nesbit's farm. These neighbors had become accustomed to living with hundreds of cats. Somewhere before or after, they put arsenic-laced ground hamburger out by their corn cribs to kill the ridiculous amount of rats, who were not afraid of the cats. Apparently!

All over the county, near and far, came reports of farm dogs becoming ill and dying. I found my beloved collie lying on the front lawn, cold as the earth he lay on.

It was not long until everyone who lose farm dogs heard of the stupidity of a place with too many cats, rats, and arsenic-laced ground beef for the taking.

Somewhere a Place

May each day hold some memories of the joys,
you have to remember and find delight among the bad.

With sorrow as a companion of two hearts that were one,
may each day a reminder of how far your life has come.

The joys and the hurts are many in this life at times,
with faith, love and compassionate understanding.

Your heartaches from your loss will mend you will find,
somewhere in heaven, a place we all can go.

Be comforted by the belief in your heart,
that this is so.

Rabbit Stew

It was 1942 when the Second World War was taking place. Like many heroic young American men, my father was enlisting for freedom from world domination by Adolf Hitler and his regime's soulless conscious attack on anyone who might stand in his way.

My father was farming then. Try as he would, he was not allowed to sign up. He was told he had a heart condition and instructed to return to tend to his business because he would be dead in a few short years.

Sometime in chis time frame, he had begun raising rabbits.

The number of rabbit cages he began building needed to house nearly three hundred procreating long-eared, fussy-tailed, domesticated varmints.

In need of a quick fix after much thought, he, one by one, opened each box setting every bunny free.

In those days and earlier, people raised and hunted rabbits for food, for their pelts, and of course, that mass production of the lucky brightly colored rabbit's foot hanging on a chain. I loved mine. It was comforting in some pleasant way, furry to the touch, and came with no maintenance.

The dirt road that went by the farm soon attracted hunters with guns, killing more than a few rabbits, along with natural enemies, taking its toll-an unknown number hopefully escaped to safer terrain. Where they lived in constant danger outside those once secure cages and now were free to wander, perceived as always being perceived as someone's dinner tonight.

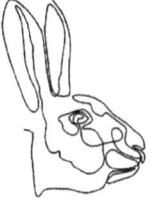

Dam-it, the Rabbit!

I had a pet rabbit named Dam-it; one day, he got out and roamed carelessly in my fenced backyard. Dam-it, I would soon find, had safely wedged himself between bags of white powdered plaster. I had been gone, and when I returned home, my dog had gotten out of the house and immediately greeted me, completely covered in the white powder from his head to his rail. When I soon discovered my side yard covered in white, looking closely, I found my rabbit hiding where my dog spent the afternoon completely removing the hair on the rabbit's butt that was hairless. The rabbit's butt was like a well-coiffed smooth shaved, perfectly groomed bald person's head, and soft like a baby's butt. The rabbit lived to see another day with no damage, rips, rears, or bite marks. I was responsible and did what we all should do: I found my pet rabbit a perfect new home. In the regards to pets, please know that the world we have is the world we have, until pet owners allow the gentleness of so many animals like a person's soul, wither and die painful deaths are soulless with no mind-heart-soul connection. Doing the right things in your life will begin to prop up your soul, so others, as well as yourself, will notice that taking flight begins with the freedom to believe there is nothing a healthy soul cannot accomplish.

Walking a Thin Line

Is it that hard to understand why any of us could at any moment be walking a thin line of stress? Regrettably, you again hit bottom, time after time, so on and so forth. The good news is you will survive the fall because you were already near the bottom long ago, man y times! Tell me, if this is not an accurate evaluation of who you are. I can find hope that some life's work out better then so many that seem not too.

So, if you are manic depressed, having mood swings, and lacking in why you are sad or angry. So me goo d news is that you can recognize who you were in the past and erase years of programming yourself to that very place you are. It is the same for a lot of us, as one in five people will become mentally ill this year alone.

Most of us have a sense of what its mean's to be overly stressed and sometimes lagging to keep up with life's challenges. Others seem more capable of towing a heavy load without breaking down and becoming stressed out-the feelings of overload. Having little energy is, at best, "so, so" and not getting any better as you wonder where this current down in the dumps will lead and whether it will ever just go away. The answer is no!

If we could be more like this and less like that, we could be more like a sloth or become more like the red fire ant. Depression is like a slow• moving sloth, while a red fire ant has a different plan. {Fire ants can kill you very quickly.} We will use these two creatures as the differential, the scale of more like one of these and less like the other. Stop and take a brain test of your life, past, present, and future—rate from red fire ant 1 to 10 and the slow-moving sloth from 10 to 1. You might seem to get a realistic answer to who you are on that scale. Make all the excuses you want. Good or bad, your reasoning has you be who you have been and who you are now, so I ask you to pause. Give yourself a better tomorrow.

A stream of millions of red fire ants, driven to attack and conquer, parade endlessly to and fro, while high up above in the safe canopy of the jungle, the sloth is safe and goes unnoticed. Being reclusive is sometimes the best way to live.

Life can be likened to a daily swim in an Amazon river full of life threatening crocodiles, flesh eating piranhas, twenty foot snakes, not forgetting those disgusting blood sucking leeches which adheres themselves to the flesh of the unconscious morsel enjoying his swim.

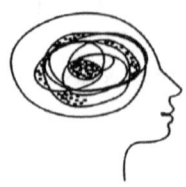

Mental Health

Toxicity, Truth, or Dare

The truth is that millions of people in the United States are on medicines for the mental depression disease. In the United States of America, one in six people are prescribed anti-depressants, and white Americans are at the top of the list. In comparison, minorities and the less fortunate are not as likely to seek help; therefore, they are left to suffer from the symptoms of being mentally ill.

Of those who are healthier, four out of five people are responsible for being conscious of those in their lives who may need help. Search for organizations and places in most cities to seek someone to listen to those who need to talk. It is not your job to fix anyone; it is our job to be more compassionate to that one in five who needs help. Be aware that your kindness is what you have to offer. There is no one answer to understanding the mind and how it is a vital part of being human. Our world spins around inside our heads and is easily affected when negative energy seems to pull at every turn.

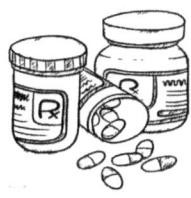

Anti-depressants or Anti-pills

We all know of others who have died of overdoses, those who have died from liver disease from drinking-all the deaths of years of substance abuse that run rampant in our psychopath world. None of this will end for those dying souls every day with little mental connects between their mind-heart connection. Insanity is a bi-product from not living authentically to your given possibility, your unconscious choices, the sane are left to ponder.

The bad news is that if you are one of the countless people struggling with habitual, chronic, unhealthy behavior, using illegal drugs that have not been prescribed, there is a renewed opportunity in seeking professionals to help any of us. It would be such a Godsend to so many desperate families that are hopeless and left feeling helpless. In this book, my conversation about mental illness is for any individual identifying with suffering from mental depression that may lead to a perpetual mental disorder by illuminating all our dark places in our mind-heart-soul.

Fractions? No, not a math question but a whodunit mystery. I'm dealing with life as it seems to deal with me "randomly!" A person's life can be divided into pieces, like a pie, cut into many individual parts. Your daily life is like a roulette wheel, and you spin it hoping to land on something that will keep you turning the wheel and playing this game called life! Unfortunately, if the entire pie is loaded with torment, anxiety, fear, and reluctance, it is hard to find contentment and joy. We are all capable to start baking a better pie. While doing ourselves a big favor, redo your game wheel.

It is all too difficult for those suffering a life time of depression. We are always in a mind game, and we seldom find comfort in how we feel each day. Any form of anxiety without behavioral control leads to deeper, more permanent fears and, of course, the dreaded pressure will drive you crazy.

The following illustration might be best exercised if we draw a big circle on paper. Next, list all your life concerns, the stuff that drives you crazy. Those nagging irritants, real or unreal, keep you feeling like life is a chore and its always time to milk the cow! While waiting for someone to bring you a milkshake.

Your list might be short or very long. Do a thorough job of all the random craziness in your mind, heart, and soul Now start to cut your circle into pieces. Dividing your 12-inch pie into as many slices as needed before you realize this will never work! Admitting you need a bigger pie or two bigger pies?

Now that you are gaining insight into the animal you have become, living in your jungle. All those things you listed and sectioned into slices in your twenty-four-hour day are impossible and at least overwhelming in the best of situations. Overwhelming is the tip of the iceberg: all the anxiety about all that stuff you have little to no control over. The things you wake up to each morning and go to bed with each night.

Vanilla or Chocolate

The number of choices we gee in a lifetime is immeasurable. For most of us, the option of choice is not very easy! For those who have difficulty choosing, you are giving up your power for what reason? Soon not only will people begin to choose for you, but you will always need to regain your footing while relying on others. We train others how to treat us. Years of teaching everyone in your life has a definition of who you are and how you show up. How we show up only changes if we show up as changed. Good luck. No one changes. Or do they?

No One Changes

Yes, it's mostly true. People don't change because we won't let them. Out of the blue, anyone can move to a new city to start over. The problem is we can either sink or swim. Although differently than before, back when life had too many corners in your round world. Back then, when insanity was a thing that was stalking you in the shadows. It should have no room or place with the here and the now. You have moved on! Unfortunately, it's the only change of clothes you brought with you. To have *different,* you have to do differently. For some, life can be as easy as a change of clothing. Because, yes, it just might be the people around you that cause your mental stress. Not forgetting that "crazy is as crazy does!" You can decide to run away from it all. There may be lots of people glad to see you gone. I believe that mental illness and the manic depression of those around us affect those who have or deal with its causes.

I hope you think how dumb it was to say that no one ever changes; we know that is not true. What is the truth? Given enough time! Everything, sometimes, changes. So let us concentrate on rescuing one person at a time. If you need to save more than yourself, tell them to get a book to read! You know the old saying, "Teach a person to swim and know at least that one life lived to tell the story," Or something like that! Help yourself before saving others. Depression leads to drowning because they cannot mentally keep their heads above water.

Significantly, those you are most involved with daily, do not help save you but drag you down with them. Craziness is everywhere; look for a place to calm your mind-heart-soul.

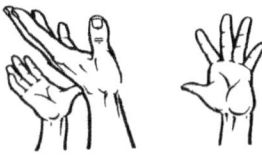

The Problem with Free Thinking

As a single entity, the moment we can acknowledge that we mentally exist is where it all begins. Consciousness takes root. At that moment, we begin to internally program our thinking, learning how to play the game of life. We all developed with different life situations.

The psychology of the family you are born into determines the cognitive thinking of individuals coming out of that environment! The outcome is as infinite as the world population's past, present and future! What and who you are as an adult might be due to your inability to change your behavior, because of having lack of interest.

{Been there, done that marching band music}

Guilty or More Guilty

Just try to rationalize that any crazy thinking on your part is the other's guy's fault.

Now that we agree it's not your fault, the biggest problem is you accomplished very little in your ability to see things like they are.

Impossible! You have similar issues as millions of other people struggling to do the impossible. People like you who live with depression and anxiety need to get diagnosed and prescribed medication. Speaking with a therapist and good counseling does help in a world that seems somehow tipped upside down. To so many of us, we do the impossible every day, and it is causing immeasurable damage to our ability to relax or slow down. Give yourself a break and let others know you are experiencing mental illness, up-close and personal each day.

Let's Pretend

Please give it up. Pretending is like having imaginary chickens in the imaginary chicken coup you never built, but still get up every day and loo k for imaginary eggs.

On the other hand, daydreaming is a great diversion, and it helps keep our minds relaxed and in balance while we escape life's craziness that will soon relentlessly dump us back into the real world.

I get up in the mornings with a fresh-brewed java in hand, and I go to the back porch, where I sit my cup down, and the birds anxiously await their breakfast. Each morning I fill up a lo ng rectangular tray on top of my patio wall. Then I sit down to watch the birds go at it. Unfortunately, for all the others, one dominating male dove shows up first, then not letting other bird s get to the seeds in the tray. He attacks all the other doves who dare try to eat with his wings held high in a slapping motion. With all that fighting going on soon, all the birdseed is on the ground. The birds are left to forage on the ground, along with the full-cheeked ground squirrels who quickly haul the day's seeds deep into their boroughs before they are game for the other predators like cats. Evidence of dead birds is the feathers scattered about the ground. Well, no thing about life should surprise us. We all need to eat!

Nor to be outwitted by a bird brain, I put out three feeders with seeds! The bullying bird, now confused about what feed to defend, gave up his battle.

The moral of this story is when he was outwitted; he now was just another irritating bird who was no longer causing havoc in the lunchroom.

Second morale: When you spend too much time keeping other birds from getting anything to eat, your reward may eventually lead the bully to starve to death!

A Christmas Without Santa

Some don't believe in Christmas others say Santa isn't real,
but I know up close and personal that Santa Claus has been ill.
Yes, we all are getting older, and Santa is undoubtedly much older too,
thank goodness for those elves; you know Santa's Christmas crew!

He runs the operation from his condo near the beach,
with the latest computer equipment and a cell phone at arm's reach.
He hasn't been very steady, and he falls about every day,
he blames it on his eyesight, mostly his feet get in the way.

Some days Santa can't remember, those winters filled with snow;
I shouldn't tell you this, he'd feel bad to have you know.
Bur Santa hasn't felt real good, and his condo it needs work,
some days, he can't seem to find his panes; he doesn't know where to look.

He spends most days just thinking if I were young again,
he gets lost in all those memories of all those Christmas he's done.
He whittles at his pencil and hums a Christmas song,
speed dials 1-800-north pole, curious to hear how it's coming along!

Mrs. Claus, she's not in the kitchen,
she doesn't like to cook!
Instead, she'd rather be at the beach,
sunbathing and reading a good book.

She loves wearing her bikini and eats lots of junk food,
she always wears her sunscreen, tries hard to read, but she mostly sleeps.
Santa hates the sand she brings to bed each and every night,
but he doesn't say a word and patiently waits to turn off the light.

Some nights he thinks of Christmas,
just before he's drifting off to sleep.
Most nights, he's just thankful,
he's got his Mrs. Claus smelling of the beach.

Santa's health may be slipping but not enough to see,
any loss of his Christmas spirit in his hours decorating the tree.
The joy in life "like Christmas," each moment of each year,
can be made of celebration, filled with Christmas cheer.

John P. Kaufman 1996-2022

Life is Like the Cactus

Life is like the cactus, so full of prickly pains,
she offers us existence and takes away the same.
When surrounded by her presence, we tread in safe pursuit,
we dare not touch her needles, and her stings are hurting proof.

Life has its barren moment, The cacti have the same,
in honesty, there always come some truths and lats of pain.
The dessert is her landscape, we find her painted there,
the days of beauty are numbered so short a time each year.

Looking at the desert cactus,
her hurt, the scabbing pain, her jab,
It knows if her beauty comes but once,
her natural beauty out-weights all her bad.

We know the mighty struggle to survive the desert sun,
her hope for eternal life, her wait for spring to come.
Life is like the cacti, some bloom each spring, and some die,
the beauty begins by enjoying them with a loving eye.

John Kaufman
Written 4/25/1982 In memory of Larry Peters, May He Rest in Peace.

Undying Love

If I should die tomorrow,
I would wait at heaven's door.
With open arms to greet you,
with more love than sand on sandy shore.

If measured by appreciation,
our time together would never end.
I commit to you my undying love,
that is the message I send.

If you should die tomorrow,
I know not what I would do.
You are my hopes, *my* world,
unimaginable without you.

Two souls became entwined forever,
when no rhythm or reason was given.
Our all-knowing love-filled journey,
life, death, our spirits eternal living.

John Kaufman February 17, 2004

From Here to Nowhere

Old looking young men, hot but cold, and church steps going nowhere, nowhere. Who am I, only nothing? Here I am, something, but that equals nothing, somewhere else or nowhere else, whatever the case may be. Old-looking young men just looking, hot but cold, feeling warm, and church steps going nowhere, nowhere. Who are you? Something, somewhere, but that equals nothing if you don't know where somewhere is, and even if somewhere is somehow here, it's actually nothing, nowhere, or somehow nothing somewhere. Cigarette machines not being able to give you cigarettes. Feeling happy but sad, I mean sad but happy, or, instead just feeling okay. Besides, where does it get a guy but nowhere, nowhere? Just a big hand in the sky, which equals something, somewhere but somehow equals nothing, nowhere or something, somewhere, equaling one big nothing right here. But if that's the case, it is something somehow right here, notnothing, not something, just not! Just two nothings or somethings, equaling something or nothing, somehow, somewhere, whatever the case may be.

John Kaufman - 1972 first published in my book: *Messages from God - The Complicated Road to Sainthood*

Stupidity and the Soul

It's not how smart you may think you are! It's how dumb your life assumes you can be. Assuming you are intelligent. The good news is smart dumb or otherwise having a good soul lasts for an eternity, long after your ability to connect the docs from where your journey began and to where your eternity will take you. Consciously preparing for your personalized inevitable future, either with a health y soul or one you unconsciously paid little attention to, success comes when you have a three dimensional mind-heart-soul connection.

Every individual life comes with life changing machinery, it is your job, not anyone else's to gain the wisdom of self. Helping light humanity's darkness to a place where the mind-heart-soul is propelled to where eternity is patiently waiting to feel your gloriously light adorned soul.

Mr. Fix-It!

Dedicated to Gayle Lorraine Kaufman Peters

She was the epitome of a strong-willed lady who ever lived. She was so loved by all that were blessed to have known her.

We celebrate her glorious life of living, along with her eternal, bright beautiful soul

My sister Gayle was terrific at almost everything,
she always worked full- time and had a fix-it repair business as well,
I designed her business cards for her,
"Why Hire a Super Man when a Wonder-Woman works."

They call you Mr. Fix-it because we know you can,
although you are female, you' re better than any man.
They call you M r. Fix-it; by that, we mean no harm,
whenever there is trouble, Gayle, come fix it, our holler of alarm.

Although, you're seldom perfect,
your work is quite superb.
You mean so much to many,
from so many we have heard.

You always set the standard of how we all should be,
oh, Gay le, can you fix it? oh, pretty, pretty, please.
They call you Mr. Fix-it a name that fits so well,
if ever you can't fix it, it was probably shot to hell!

With life, there comes some wisdom,
something we all should learn.
When we're having trouble fixing things,
to know where we can turn.

A Letter With a Junk Store Cat

My grandma's name was Elsie, and I loved her a lot.
So, when I saw this naked kitty-cat on a thrift store shelf,
I rescued her quickly as I could, and I decided to name her,
Miss Elsie Da-Puddy-Cat!

So, on this day, I give you,
to keep, care for, and to love.
A junk store find, with you in mind,
to say how much your thought of.

Some cats' fur is messy,
matted and shaggily worn.
I found her in a plastic bag,
where she was born.

Naked, "Miss Elsie the Da-Puddy-Cat,"
she needs some loving care.
So could you, with your sewing machine,
make her something purdy to wear!

A dress that is so purdy,
with lots of frilly embroideries.
A constant example, a reminder of,
how a purdy a Puddy-Cat can be.

John Kaufman - August 19, 2002

All of those birthday cards from my lifetime of personal poems written for those souls near and dear to my mind-heart-soul.

A Happy Birthday Poem for My Aunt Ardis

I've just invented ancestral eyeglasses,
how do I know this is so?
Why, put them on for a short time,
and you will surely know.

Now my great granddaddy,
he could drink some of his hill-Billie brew.
But grandma drank as much as he,
say those that say they knew.

It seems most of our aunts and uncles
loved drinking day and night.
Inherited that double vision thing,
screw-in up their doggone sight.

Our family line goes back hundreds of years,
and we dig up lots of old bones; it's true.
Bue with these eyeglasses, you will see
aunts and uncles, you never knew.

Our family, they were many,
came from somewhere in Ireland over there.

The living was mighty rough at times,
sometimes it called for beer.

With alcohol and having kids,
our family's accomplishment is pretty clear.
Let us be happy they drink a bit,
or, we might not be here.

Now I've invented these eyeglasses,
so that you can have a peak.
Put a rest to all those questions,
about those aunts and uncles you seek.

So, with these brand-new eyeglasses,
I hope your vision remains crystal clear.
If you should develop double vision,
unlike many others, I hope it's not severe.

1995

Happy Birthday, Dad

I never knew any real cowboys,
that did not love to be riding the range.
A rope, a saddle, their styl'in outfits,
they are always fancy, seldom plain.

I wonder what they're dreaming,
most days, just riding that horse.
It's supposed to be a mystery,
to all of us un-cowboys, of course!

We can only pray each day of each year,
in the life of a cowboy, is better than the last.
With a new hard riding adventure waiting,
for him around his next unexplored pass.

With all that cow boys do, a rid-din', and rope-in,
constantly chewing on something, ooh!
I know that getting older is one something,
you cowboys don't have any interest to do.

June 27, 1995

Birthday-Cake-Ice-Cream-Mom

It was long ago on an old dusty trail,
and I'll never forget it, I remember it well.
Our stagecoach was surrounded,
and mother looked worried and turning pale.

The bad guys were winning this game,
that these outlaws had begun.
So, I got mother our of the coach,
and we began to run.

The dust was a blow-in',
and the skies were as dark as night.
But mother and I kept running,
we had no guns to fight!

It was pretty scary, a really bad dream,
I just kept yelling to mother, don't be afraid.
Think of something extra-ordinary,
like birthday cake and ice cream.

This story is a good one and close to being true,
we made it back to safety,
swear-in' if we made it back,
what we would do.

Now every year about this time we celebrate,
doing precisely what we said.
We eat some cake and ice cream,
then we go to bed.

When I talk about this story,
people always seem to say,
what's your favorite ice cream?
How's your mom today?

Why my mom is as good as ever,
it's chocolate swirl delight, I reply.
Wha t good is any story,
with the truth, there is no lie.

The moral of this story is as simple as can be,
when you find yourself in trouble,
just run for cake and ice cream,
it worked for mother and me!

LoveYou, Mom
John Kaufman

Goodnight for Christmas

'Twas the night before Christmas, at ho me in my house,
with plenty to eat, not much to complain about.
My dogs Cody and Carmen were asleep on my bed,
while visions of beef jerky danced in their heads.

I ran to the window knowing Santa would soon appear,
hoping for once, his sleigh would stop here!
I was wearing silk boxers, or was it winter underwear?
It doesn't matter, as I sat there upset, trying not to swear.

I have been waiting to meet Santa for far too many years,
now I've heard Santa's story, how "lively and quick,"
after too many years of waiting,
could this be a cruel trick?

His big rosy cheeks, his face covered in curly white hair,
flying reindeer with antlers and Santa himself for proof.
I stare at the chimney with some hope for a thrill,
glancing at Santa's cookies, half sleeping, I sit very still.

Waiting for this guy dressed head to his feet,
I expect him to be covered in black ash like a chimney sweep.
If I can't have stuff that he carries in his sack,
how about money to help pay for all this expensive Christmas crape?

Money makes my eyes twinkle, so full of joy,
how about a bunch of cash for this old boy?
"More rapid than eagles, his coursers they came,"
I'm becoming suicidal, and Mother Goose is to blame.

Now I've eaten his cookies like a chubby little elf,
and I've eaten them all despite my not-so-great health.
It's late, and I'm tired and want to go to bed,
the thought Santa was not coming twirled around in my head.

I'm grumpy and irritated that the holidays are finally here,
just another Christmas without Santa and his flying reindeer.
The family is coming to visit and soon will be here,
gathering together full of love, joy, and holiday cheer.

So let us be happy and celebrate the season that's here,
always believing in Santa and his flying reindeer.
May your heart stay full with love and holiday cheer,
each enjoying this time of each year.

John Kaufman 1983

Stuff to Consider!

As life was in severe decline, the older man crossed the road to get his mail, but once again, there was no mail because there was no mailbox.

Like his soul, the lack of consciousness will forever be searching for that mailbox he will never be able to find!

My mother went to assisted living each night; she packed a bag to go home and waited by the door for Jack, her deceased husband, to pick her up. He had been dead for ten years.

Waiting is such a notoriously boring place to get on with it!

Your interpretation of your consciousness may result from your inability to focus consciously.

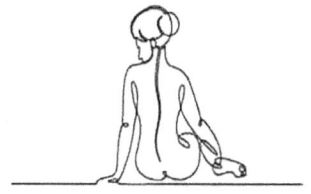

The Lessons of Self

When we rely on others to make our choices, are we weak of mind? When you need more self-worth to participate in a life with dignity, and live authentically with a purpose. If you suffer from having little self-worth, it happens when those who should have cared enough to have taken notice, but never did would have made life different for you.

Good, bad, or indifferent, it is what it is until it isn't.

An Unloving Family Will Always Equal Loneliness!

As a token of my appreciation for the endearing blessings called family in a family, as in a jigsaw puzzle, each piece plays an equally important part in creating the picture entirely as a whole.

Understanding the power of each individual piece grants the wisdom, knowledge, and vision of being not just a single part but the beauty of being part of the possibility of it a ll.

John Kaufman
From my book: " How to make Family Coloring Book."

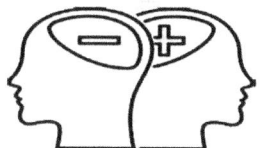

Sounds of Random Negativity

Let each of us determine where each of us is on the random scale of a person's natural disposition.

Happy and content, most days, you remain calm, optimistic, passive, and highly hopeful.

Juxtaposed, opposed somewhere near or far from life's joy is joylessness.

Feelings that life's dissatisfactions often create aggression, showing up mild and controlled or often leading to uncontrolled boldness.

Where are you when it comes to naturally feeling mean, cantankerously hopeless, indifferent in the art of being friendly to those you encounter in all, some, or most aspects of your life?

Having negative characteristics puts you among the humans who are likely ill-natured and have negative chinking, becoming dangerous to yourself and others! Changes of heart, the deterioration, loss of your soul's ability to survive without more attention to who you choose to be and not to be.

Showing compassion to yourself and others, regardless of who they are. People with a wide range of negative emotional distinctions can eventually lead any of us to develop stigmatic chronic mental illness.

Befuddled thinking can become un-befuddled with a mentor's help!

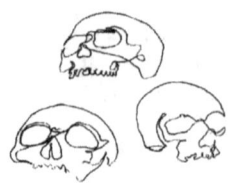

Sun Bleached Bones

Lost at sea, a row boat full of sailors, each dying one after the other, continues its voyage with the smell of rotting human flesh. Their souls had long departed from that wooden cradle containing the remnants of their flesh-picked, clean, sun-bleached bones. And unlike the descending of their souls, leaving behind wreckage, no longer needed, lost forever at the bottom of the sea.

But not! If you believe in some meta-physical hereafter. We are much better to trust that eternity is forever and all of the world's children, past, present, and future, were given a soul.

Your soul may feel lose when you find yourself floundering around lost at sea, in the dying grip of death. Go in peace, knowing you were a blessing, a bright light, to those who loved you. Letting loose the shackles that no longer are burdened in our lives.

No longer tethered to what once was, our earthly needs are not needed now. Free of life's blessings, exchanged for an eternally blessed destination, a new place forever!

Believe it or not.

{One hundred white doves winging overhead!}
John Kaufman 2022

Fifty Years and Counting

Mom and Dad's Fiftieth Anniversary
The poem I wrote for them.—July 22, 1995

Cupid with his arrow,
drew back his bow and shot,
after fifty years of marriage,
he must have hit the spot.

We'll talk about the good times
and not of any bad,
life has some of both.
You made it and we're glad.

We'll dance around the table,
hoot, and holler, and shout it out.
We really love the two of you,
that's what this hollering is about.

There has never been a couple,
with all you both possess.
The two of you have made it,
when life puts you to the test.

Our hearts are filled with joy,
to celebrate your life together.
We have traveled near and fur,
our lives with you in it, is better.

We will love you both forever,
from every bit of laughter.
To every joyous heartfelt tear.
we are happy to be here.

Now, this isa new beginning,
a day to have some fun.
After fifty years together,
this is no time to run.

So, thanks to Cupid's arrow,
he indeed struck you two.
After fifty years together,
celebrating is all there is to do.

The Rest of Your Life

It's the day before the rest of your life.
What are your actions and reactions,
as you stand there while your days slip away,
like water through badly cupped hands?

Life needs joys like the flower need bees,
and the nectar is never seen nor casted,
if winter cloaks our soul and summer,
doesn't warm our heart s anymore.

Joylessness is created when landscapes become barren,
and there is but snow on the ground.
No blossoms or bees are around us anymore,
and any taste or sweet nectar is go ne.

When life becomes riddled with dark thunderstorms,
inspiration can come in the smallest of forms.
Look in new places from deep within the heart,
sometimes the end is the best place to start.

May your field of flowers become many,
each bee in your life a sweet honeycomb makes.
May each season be filled with a life of joy,
and your blessings always outweigh life's mistakes!

Feelings, needs, and wants left untouched and neglected are frostbite to the soul.

John Kaufman Original Poem: Messages from God

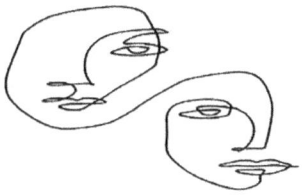

The Soul-Spiritual-Connection

I have been communicating with higher spirits nearly every day of my life. Did any deities notice me screaming when I was in pain or afraid of this world? Hiding behind furniture most of my life when I could feel safer there. Our planet, most living things, including global warming are suffering the effects of feeling life is out of control with anxiety disorders, and a growing number of people who could use some help. While I took a psychology class in college, we occasionally went outside and had the class meet in the shade of a giant oak tree. After class was over, the professor pulled me aside, and as I looked into her face perplexed, she asked me why I was always avoiding her line of easy vision. What was my thinking? I don't remember what I told her. I have always known why I have hidden behind over-stuffed furniture, and I have become quite good at it! I hoped the professor and everyone else could and would see I could have been more intelligent. My mind-heart-soul was convinced to believe what I had been told my entire life, reasons to hate myself. I had the most beautiful heart, with a brain that constantly told me to hide, crying nor to provoke the pain I felt most every day by my always feeling so stupid.

Insanity reigns in those wandering through their life without heart-soul domination in some people's minds produces what none of us like to see or hear. The constant sounds of rusty metal grinding in our thinking produces mostly a scenario no one wants to hear.

None of My Business

Your fears, lack of crust, the inhumanity of it all, too many of us living with suspicions and suspect of everyone we avoid meeting. The way of the world makes us tread lightly for the safety of survival in this life we have been given.

Worth is the imaginary value each of us assigns to our made-up opinions. Where you invest your time, money, life, and eternity is none of my business.

If my soul is like a bag of buttery popcorn, there will always be un-popped kernels in the journey of a life lived. Get over it!

For all those things we may not like about who we are, a sad song will hold little joy. A good soul can survive and can endure for the soul's sake. What appears to us may not be apparent, and no one is above natural law. Such as, in Putin's Russian attacks against Ukraine, evil souls can be a horrible thing, dark and relentless.

The epitome of a mentally unconscious demonic soul will always be part of humanity's reality. Those rulers of such darkness will always be enemies that test the soul. Lay traps for us to stumble upon, helpless in understanding their meaning.

Life will get you down. How much? Maybe all of it! I have fought depression all my life, still. I still shine as one of the kindest authentic souls. I am blessed to love and appreciate my mind-heart-soul relationship.

No matter the reason, I have felt all alone and primarily alone for most of my life. Still! For most of my life, there was me. The thinking was a conversation with myself in my head nonstop. I laugh at my jokes, and people laugh with me; it does the soul good!

I was born a Gemini, and I can do nothing without logic. Like a soul that can do nothing without questioning everything until I am satisfied or lose crack of my thoughts.

I have traveled such a long way in understanding the destination of my truths, a journey through the twisted jungles of humanity's mind. Life's journey is far more enthralling and valuable when your mind-heartsoul connection is responsible for your three-dimensional soul's unstoppable dynamics.

{Sounds of unstoppable constructive dynamics.} John Kaufman - 2022

One Hundred Percent Organic

A Soul, its religious or non-religious content, is continuously downloaded from the thinking brain to our unconsciousness. Authenticity becomes the belief in our contents, and it listens to our words, what we speak, and the emotions from each heart by executing a conscious connection from you that is the pure light of the soul. There is this enormous world of self-expression by finding the soul and defending its eternal value; life-changing.

Categorical Speaking: Let's pretend we were born a duck. You know you will soon find that you can shuffle your webbed feet on land, in water, and get airborne when needed.

Think like a duck, walk like a duck; you're not. You are much, much more than that! We come into this world where the noise becomes much louder. Until somewhere in mid-life, hopefully much sooner on a three-dimensional stable foundation. You are lucky if you are surrounded by people who can speak from the heart to their minds and choose to respond in some light instead of darkening negativity.

So told are the storms that come by me, as winter frostbite does to fragile things. When you try to overlook looking, the damage shows up **in the** soul.

I am dear-minded when I say all souls and their religious connections start with the heart and mind, which soon begins to enhance and modify the soul's consciousness.

There is a saying, "we are what we eat." Said another way, you are responsible for a healthy soul.

Eyes of an Old Dog

What would any old dog look like who had little love, shelter, food, or water; a reflection, in his dark, hopeless gaze into empty abyss? Will your end times be dark and full of voids? That is how your soul will feel without the heart, mind and soul connection. Freedom for a while, maybe, until your choices have left: your souls tuck for eternity in a mud bog, where you finally realize that you have been your own worst enemy.

Most people have good or bad intuition.

A great mind-heart-soul connection will become how the heartless begin to have a heart through their soul's conversations, redefining their lives.

If you are honest with who you are, your authenticity of self, sooner than later, gains you the wordliness of maintaining spiritual life in the hereafter.

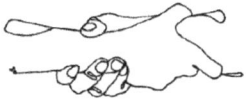

Domination

I am very clear about all those times, even now, that a battle ensues between my heart and mind. My purest heart always protected my soul-self, and it won all my wars. Despite my life of frustrations, hollering, and my brain's lack of understanding. Insanity reigns in those wandering through their life without heart-soul domination.

One's chosen religious identity might be treasured as a Holy commodity—a slippery slope for humanity. Our glory will not come from the glorious toting of religious doctrine. But from your commitment to having a magnificent soul. Regardless of any thought s, otherwise.

The Monkey and the Snake

Monkeys, like humans, are intelligent and capable of causing chaos at any moment or situation. These mammals are more interested in their well-being and success than anyone hanging around the complicated jungle forest. Like the Monkey who descends from the treetops, searching for fallen fruit on the ground, once he has found fruit, his first action is to scream Snake! He can now enjoy the fruits of his labor.

{Horrific Monkey screaming}

He screams that he has seen a snake. Every Monkey near and far hears his warning cries and races to the top of the jungle in fear. He is now left to enjoy the tasty, sweetened fruit without being taken away by all the many hungry other monkeys. The human, like the Monkey, is no different. Both can ruthlessly deceive and conceive of situations to fool others, repeatedly, without feeling any remorse for their bad behavior. Soullessness is humanity's poison. We must always try our best to pay close attention to others who, by their nature, are a danger to all of us.

To Love or Not to Love

I often say I love everyone until I meet them, ending with a little giggle. I know my soul, and I know my heart. Life seldom rewards those who have souls destined to become saints. With no need for ceremony, with a few flaws my soul, in my heart, and mind is Saint worthy. Even though I am nothing to anyone, I am something to me.

Despite my life of frustrations, my hollering, and my brain's lack of understanding, "it is what it is!" Insanity reigns corrupting those among us who are wandering through their life without "mind-heartsoul connection!"

More Food for Thought

Love without compassion is a void.

To be human is the meaning of diversity.

Our world is not all soulless and hateful; there is much anger as well. In insurrections, our truth tells no lies.

Being lazy with no effort is not a sin unless eternity's gates have been locked, knowing that laziness was not your biggest fault.

Am I wrong, not to beat back, when I am being bear upon?

John Kaufman • 2022

Joy Robbers

This, short bald man showed up in my life, a soulless devil he was pretending to be an angel. This mini-story was written and sent to Philip when he was in prison, serving time for something or other! Please beware of the soulless, for they will come to your aid before most all others. Covertly feeding and feasting on whatever they can. The soulless among us without feeling any remorse, continually devouring other's good souls. I call them "Joy Robbers," a world over powered by those mindless-heartless-soulless mix of humanity's answer to nothing, this is a tale of a heartless soulless illusion of a man.

My Dark Twisted Jungle

Another day somewhere deep in the urban jungle, a man is hacking away at the relentless forest he sees before him. Alone except for those memories of days gone by, those roads not taken, when we all were rich in pudding cups. When the days had the smell of happiness floating through the air, followed by the aroma of freshly baked brownies. None of that matters now, continuing desperately to hack noisily at the dense entangled vines that had been there long before I showed up! I clutched my machete in my left hand, my other hand covered in water-filled blisters. My feet were bleeding from the painful jungle rot that was spreading. The only thing keeping me going was my search for the remote lost city of "Drugs-Sex-Rock and Roll!" It has been commonly believed to be a mystical island for the lost and mindless in society. My left hand is now covered in blisters, but I cannot give up. I am on a mission. Looking for something to remove my mental pain, why can't I find that place they call "Drugs-Sex-Rock and Roll ?" Looking back to see my journey so far, but there was nothing to see. This jungle I am in has already left my path invisible, gone! Like the choices one makes somehow predict my hell here in this place I am. At this age, one might think I would be hopelessly defeated here in a jungle that is taking my flesh and bones to feed my demon's soul. I may be tired, bleeding, and covered with jungle roe, but I know I am close to finding "Drugs-Sex-Rock and Roll!" I will not give up, not now!

Picking up the dull, trusted machete, I do what I have always done, continue to chop away at a jungle overgrown with my belief. I will get to live the rest of my life there one day, even if it only exists deep in the dark, twisted jungle of my mind.

John Kaufman

Pocket Full of Coupons

I was blessed to live on the island of Maui for some years, where I met people from all around the world who were always vacationing in what is truly paradise to me. I was involved in a support group, an organization helping those in need of assistance and fellowship. This story I share is one I keep near to my consciousness of mind.

In Maui, the cost of food and supplies can be much more costly than on the main land. So all of us living and working there knew that coupons, sales, discounts including making trades was an option, was the only way to live by being resourceful. One evening a good friend named Steven, set out to do shopping at the one larger local grocery store. His pocket was full of coupons with high hopes of successfully saving some money.

That night after Steven had returned home and his groceries were all put away, he had all the ingredients to make him one of his favorite Island meals. With a contended full belly, he cook time to call some of us friends, excited to share that he had saved over seventeen dollars at the grocery store in coupons. It was so uplifting to hear him so excited about his day of shopping success. Another day in "paradise" was over as I got ready for bed and a good night sleep. It would be the very next morning when we all started getting phone calls, letting us know Steven earlier that morning was discovered dead. He had died of a massive heart attack. Not brought on out of his happiness, rather his deadly heart decease.

{Hawaiian Music Playing in the Background}

At a Maui beach park a large crowd of all those of us gathered to celebrate his life and his passing, it was a loving tribute to his glorious soul's journey into his eternity.

The Scorpion and the Turtle

Here is my rendition of the fable "The Scorpion and The Turtle!"
Original author unknown

There once was a scorpion who had desperately pondered to find a way to cross a river. Seeing a painted turtle contented, sunning itself on a rock nearby, he approaches the dossal turtle and greets him with an unassuming, friendly hello! Then he quickly explained his dilemma and inability to cross the river and politely asked the turtle if he could get a ride on his back to safely carry him to the other side. The turtle was aware of the scorpion's reputation for its deadly sting, and the turtle shared with the scorpion his fear that he might sting him midstream. Despite the scorpion's bad reputation, he convinces the turtle that it would never happen as it would result in death by drowning not only the turtle but to himself. Believing the scorpion's answer had eliminated his fear. He let the scorpion climb on his back and began to carry his passenger across the river.

{Rumbling of thunder storms developing overhead.}

About halfway across, the scorpion, without any thought, suddenly lashes our and stings the turtle. The turtle was now in a life-threatening dilemma of its own. It was soon to lose its life, but not before asking the scorpion, who was also doomed to drown, why had he delivered the fatal sting? The scorpion, without hesitation, replied I could not stop myself. It is just my nature!

Messages From God

The Benny Renteria Ascension Story

It is a dream come true, high-up on my bucket list to publish my poems, and an assortment of my creative artwork. One of a kind "The Three-Dimensional-Soul" is available to readers around the world. I invite readers to read my last book, "Messages From God: The Complicated Road to Sainthood." The book includes the true scenario of my witnessing the passing of my dear friend Benny. It was a meaningful blessing to have witnessed the miracle of his life, death and his gloriously departing soul. He spoke to me saying, "I've been waiting for you to wake up!" In those brief moments I was spiritually chosen to experience in his ascension. I do my best to tell the story of Benny, the moments before and after his death. It changed my mindheart-soul about death and dying.

What I witnessed has changed my conscious interpretation of the true power of the soul. The book is a must read for those who might doubt the power needed and attention in maintaining a healthy individual soul. If "Messages From God," does not create a conversation in your mind-heart-soul, maybe you are one of those nice people who are hopefully enjoying life. Living is only half of humanity's problem, dying, and death without a mind-heart-soul connection is like your attempt to hitch hike somewhere that will not welcome you even if should find it.

Our listening to the uniqueness of each individual belief can enlighten the thinking and the understanding of our own three-dimensionalsoul, we are responsible for its eternal life long after you stopped roaming the earth seeking truths that required more attention than humanity could provide. Benny had wasted away and death was upon him. He looked health y, happy, youthful, and the most holy image one could only imagine. The bolts of light shooting from his eyes and mouth as he spoke to me as I witnessed his Ascension.

What is the spiritual meaning of Ascension?

The term spiritual Ascension means a magical awakening of your soul into a higher level of consciousness. It is a vibration frequency that generates positive energy and light. It unleashes your innate powers and wisdom. The ascension is an evolutionary process that is multidimensional and confusing.

The-Three-Dimensional-Soul-Mind-Heart-Soul-Connection
John P. Kaufman 2023

www.ingramcontent.com/pod-product-compliance
Lightning Source LLC
Chambersburg PA
CBHW052150070526
44585CB00017B/2057